Sings the Body

poems by

Cindy Washabaugh

Finishing Line Press
Georgetown, Kentucky

Sings the Body

Copyright © 2016 by Cindy Washabaugh
ISBN 978-1-63534-026-6 First Edition
All rights reserved under International and Pan-American Copyright Conventions.
No part of this book may be reproduced in any manner whatsoever without written permission from the publisher, except in the case of brief quotations embodied in critical articles and reviews.

ACKNOWLEDGMENTS

Grateful acknowledgment is made to the following publications in which these poems, some in earlier versions, first appeared:

"Dream: The Pond," and "The Strands are Twisted Gold and Black," *Blue Unicorn.*
"Journal Entry, Another Birthday, 3:24 a.m.," *Coal City Review.*
"Skin, A Lament," *Confrontation.*
"Song of Grief, Arranged for Woodwinds," *Hunger Mountain.*
"329 Miles Northeast, Woman Ponders Pain's Sweetness," *Poem.*
"Breasts," and Quiet, Quiet, Lyrical Miracle," *Slipstream.*
"Cancerian Woman Leaves Her Home," "Certain Men of the Early Twenty-first Century," "Song of Yearning: Fox and Hens," "Night Song: Pachyderm," and "Night Song: Embracing the Simian," *Spoon River Poetry Review.*
"Pink," in the Anthology, *Cleveland in Prose and Poetry.*
"For Pam, Who Can't Remember," in the Anthology, *Kiss Me Goodnight.*

Publisher: Leah Maines

Editor: Christen Kincaid

Cover Art: *Bee Tara* by Donna Iona Drozda © Wren House Studio
http://www.donnaionadrozda.com

Author Photo: Stephanie Trzaska

Cover Design: Elizabeth Maines

Printed in the USA on acid-free paper.
Order online: www.finishinglinepress.com
also available on amazon.com

Author inquiries and mail orders:
Finishing Line Press
P. O. Box 1626
Georgetown, Kentucky 40324
U. S. A.

Table of Contents

I

Pink 1
Juno's Song: Field Trip to the Health Education Museum 2
Dream: The Pond... 3
Quiet, Quiet, Lyrical Miracle 4
Night Song: Pachyderm 5
Dream of Bees.. 6
Breasts 7
Night Song: Incubation... 8
For Pam, Who Can't Remember 9
The End of Bees 10
Night Song: Embracing the Simian 11

II

The Familiar 14
Certain Men of the Early Twenty-first Century 15
Song of Yearning: Fox and Hens.. 16
Last Rites.. 17
The Strands are Twisted Gold and Black............................. 18
She Measures Life in Thin Slices... 19
Daughter at the Edge: Doan Brook Gorge 20
Skin: A Lament 21
Song of Grief, Arranged for Woodwinds 22

III

What We Know.. 24
329 Miles Northeast: Woman Ponders Pain's Sweetness..... 25
The Life I Never Lived With My Sister Pam 26
Journal Entry, Another Birthday, 3:24 a.m. 27
River Song, Night Crossing... 28
Cancerian Woman Leaves Her Home 29

*With gratitude, for my mother, and
for all of the mothers, daughters, sisters,
and friends who've crowded my life with love.
And for Patrick, always.*

I

Pink

The foil star at the tip makes her leery at first, but she commands
be silent and her sister goes mute. She orders *somersault, pirouette,*

chant Twinkle Little Star. Then bored with puppeting her sister
around the living room, she pads to the porch.

On his red banana bike, David broncos past. She shakes it low,
jump the curb. He balances on his back tire, *what's with the wand?*

so she jabs it at his handlebars. *Yeah righ*t, he peals out, *how about
zapping me up a red Camaro?*

Stomach fisted, she storms inside, truly doesn't even know
what a camaro is. She slides upstairs past her sister, still perched

obedient on the couch. Toward her bedroom window
she tips the star, *make it rain.* The sky shouts blue.

On her dresser, a tiny sea shell, music box, little statue
of Mary from her Grandma. She thumbs the shell's ridged back,

bitty spot of pink inside, then nudges, *turn pink.* Kneeling
vigil on her bed, she wills the little oval to win the shell's

whole underside. It does not pink up entirely but—yes—
after a while, yes, she's certain that the center pulses bigger.

Juno's Song: Field Trip to the Health Education Museum

Like the goddess, her name was Juno. Seven-feet-tall
and transparent, she displayed her brain, intestines,

even her uterus. Elbows back, she invited us to gaze
as she turned on her silver platform. A static-y

voice, like a radio, floated *I am Juno* but her lips
were molded shut. Red and blue rivers of blood vessels

mapped her. When her spine ignited, the nerves
traveling her arms and legs flashed white, organs glowed

orange, then red, while she droned on like our librarian:
Here is my liver. And here, my pancreas. On my arm, blonde

hairs spiked up in the cold room. A brown mole starred
the shoulder of the girl next to me. Our muscles got round

when we moved so you knew they were there beneath
our skin. I traced the pale blue veins in my wrist, felt

blood beat against my fingers. Juno had none of this,
was as plain as a drink of water with her robot voice,

her thick body just a case to hold all her lit-up insides.
Even her hair was clear plastic, crimped tight. Why

did they even name her, when she wasn't
really anyone at all?

Dream: The Pond

It's two weeks since my Mom died and we hear old Mr. Jenner is trying to kill himself. When his son takes away his shotgun and goes to pick up groceries, Mr. Jenner takes his straight-edge and slashes his wrists. Then he drives his tractor into the pond at the back of his farm where we fish. I can't stop wondering whether he drowned or bled to death. An ambulance takes his wife, body rotting with tumors, though she'd never shown signs. One night I dream I'm looking into the pond and my mother drives out of it on Mr. Jenner's tractor laughing. Just this last line is the dream.

Quiet, Quiet, Lyrical Miracle

It's drizzling this morning on my new plaid dress. The rain makes it smell like bug spray, and I'm worried he'll smell it. Yesterday in Family Living, which we all know means Sex Education, the nurse said, remember "vagina" by thinking "Virginia." *That's my aunt's name*, he breathed into my hair, *I hope I don't get mixed up*. When I look up, his bus is already here and then he's walking so close by I see the freckles on his neck, the soft, white hair on the tops of his ears. And that's when it happens. Right near my hip bones, but deeper in my body, I feel two "pings" like guitar strings being plucked—just where my ovaries are—I saw it on the Family Living chart. At first I'm scared and worry it made noise, but no one's looking. So I think maybe I ovulated for the first time ever and I marvel at the power of my love for Joe Edwards, that it could turn me into a woman while I stand here in the rain.

Night Song: Pachyderm

Like a cinder block, it presses, the foot of an elephant
leaning, but not with his whole self yet. The shell-shape
of the nails surprises you, evenness of the sole's weight

along your breastbone. You try to decode some
message from the hatched lines in his hide, to read
the crazy Braille around his toes. So dark you can

just make out the pale sheen of tusks curving toward
your face. Small eyes glint farther off, fat serpent
of his trunk grazes you behind your right ear,

at your wrist, your navel, hair bristling your skin
when it brushes past. You breathe shallow in your chest
to keep from feeling the crush. If you're still, will he forget?

Remove his awful *pied* and lumber off? For now, you lie
quiet and wait for the feel, the sound of cracking,
heart thudding its muffled song beneath your ribs.

Dream of Bees

Clad in jeans only, I stand in the oak-burled parlour
of a tattered mansion. On my forearm a dozen bees hum.

Something in the amber bulge of thorax, leg-sacs stuffed
with pale dust, shimmer of wings, scrolls hieroglyphs

of buzz onto my skin. All my pulses listen, aware of the stingers
scraping, under each honeyed body, the venom sac.

Breasts

All girls, wedged in a tight ring, hip-huggers
and nylon body suits, shoes hidden under big bells,
dizzy with debate over whether Tim Marsh

really kissed Tina in study hall. We don't care,
just need to attach the hum running through us to
something. Janie tilts toward me, purple top

stretched tight over her breasts. One rubs my elbow,
reminds me of my mother, just six months since
she died. I laugh at the right times but I'm remembering

how it felt to lean on my mother's chest, my head
rising and falling. How, charged with electricity,
my hair clung to her blouse when I moved away.

The bell shrills and we scatter. In bed that night,
I think about Janie—what if she were kissing one
of the other girls—maybe Sarah, maybe Tina.

Night Song: Incubation

She skitters oily across the floor, scarab beetle,
jewel-backed queen—her feet tap a mad waltz,

her shine and patter hypnotize as she scuttles
the bed's leg, climbs your throat, shimmies

in the corner of your mouth.
Morning, thoughts buzz like obsidian beads—

your pulse a steely twang, a delicate throb
sings your ears.

Translucent and sticky, they unrolled all night,
arched off on their own to find homes—

curl grubs hatched in the soft nest of your gut.

For Pam, Who Can't Remember

Lean close, little sister and look, I carry it all in this
glad hump: stretched "o" of your mouth,

your skinny limbs, the way we flew at Dad
and he rocked us, 10 and 12, *it'll be all right, we're gonna*

be OK, while Grandma hunched over the stove
crying in the same small voice she laughed in, heating

Campbell's soup for us at 9:45 in the morning.
Here, the oil Mom painted, how we fingered the canvas,

raised brush strokes sure evidence she'd been here, moved
her hands to make a small world—blue night, ebony trees,

ghost moon smudge. One day you water-colored
your pink clouds in her sky, her dark trees sprouted

your flowers of yellow and red. Then the canvas
mildewed black, reeked like earth, so we had to

throw it away. Now, for the black that filled
your small skull that first morning, swallowed

everything around it, I open this chaimoised sack.
I welcome you into this night lit by so many stars, each one

gleaming its single story, cruel and precious and sweet.

The End of Bees

> *"People don't realize that without pollinating insects, we won't have berries on trees, and so won't have birds. If we don't have birds, it just works up the food chain."*
> —*John Chapple, Chairman, London Beekeepers Assoc., London, England*

There's an absence in the garden, no dusty thrum of wings, lilies
and zinnias choking quietly on pollen. All summer, not one child stung.

A friend with three hives says only one is filled, the others ghost towns.
The same in Ontario, Seattle, London. In a field of peppertree blossoms

near Tampa, four hundred hives down to thirty-six. No dead left—
just a fine net of fungi, bacteria, viruses, teeming. Some say

it's like AIDS, stressed bees trucked cross-country in 18-wheelers,
hives stacked deep, pollinating grapefruit in Florida,

apples in Washington state, almonds in the California valleys.
Others say pesticides, mites, even cell phones. But maybe

the bees are just tired of us, yearn to take their golden buzz and honey
somewhere else. A swarm, thousands thick, just hummed

into thinnest air, got sucked into the engine of a jet bound
for Portugal. Clogging the works like clotted cream, their tiny bodies.

Night Song: Embracing the Simian

Imagine a monkey who has left her wild home, left
a humid forest full of screeching brothers and sisters
to become your own dark sibling. You have not asked this

of her in any language you know, did not plan to share
your room again, to feel her long hairy limbs thrown
over yours when you woke in the night. But there she is.

No reasoning will send her away. When you talk,
she stares listless at your mouth, scrubby fingers picking
the creases of her body. When you sneak off and leave

her in the park, she pursues you with a passion that
shocks you, mouth wide, shrieking monkey curses,
yellow teeth glistening with the spittle of her rage.

You've thought about killing her, choking her with
a rough piece of jute, holding her head under bath water
till her spindly arms stop flapping. But something in her eyes

stops you, a softness there lays bare her strange ardor for you.
She is, after all, your own. Her loping motions parody
your gestures, her comic face mirrors your precious distress.

Invite her to your table then. Let her eat mangos, apples,
raisins, or rare meat. Let her tear at the sweet flesh
and lick her sticky fingers clean. When she is drowsy

with fullness, take her to your room. Give her the good
side of the bed, the one with the candle, rug and clock.
This time throw your limbs over her. Now, watch her sleep.

II

The Familiar
It lived under the bed for twenty years.
—Naomi Shihab Nye

No light, still it thrived like some exotic mushroom, tucked
behind the bed's oak leg, beneath where

her head lay, a thousand times shielded
from the broom. Who can say why it finally ventured out,

who can say? Perhaps it had spun tendrils into her dreams,
perhaps it had its own stygian dreams.

One morning, there it was—bright yellow and hungry
and waiting for her to tell it what to do.

Certain Men of the Early Twenty-first Century

With names like Bob and John, they rock-climb, cycle, recycle
and roll sushi. They apologize when they come first, rarely do.
They always remember to put the seat down.

They rub my feet, sing me songs, tell sad tales. Their mothers:
redirected ballerinas, burned pot roast or their bras. Their fathers
knocked back whiskey, camped at the office. Eventually someone left.

Who is this man chopping scallions and carrots in my kitchen?
Sweeping the floor while I pay my bills? The one before him taught
my daughter to play piano. Got turned on watching me snake a drain.

Last week the vegetable-chopper got that down-the-road look.
"This is starting to feel good," he moped. "No matter," I think,
"the world is full of them now."

Their sisters adore them, confide in them, wish their husbands
were like them. They talk to my cats and play Scrabble with me, adore
foreign films. "We're perfect together," they say as they drift away.

Song of Yearning: Fox and Hens

He's so orange against green rolled out
like wet paint across the field. He is sick of it,

keeps his shy back low as he crosses,
someone's bound to see his fur flaming toward

the hens' pen, tall gray fence that cloisters them—
How to conjure a way through to those pretty nuns

with red hoods, chaste bodies, tending
their ovaled altars. He takes the field's edge;

they stretch their necks, bawk-bawk soft against
the fence. If only he could see the press of their

frilled breasts, how they long for the crack of shells, rasp
of his tongue in slippery gold, his teeth against their throats.

Last Rites

*Why do we entrust to a boat the weight of a funeral urn, and
celebrate the black rose festival on amethyst coloured water?*
—Osip Mandelstam

Skimming above inky water, you pull the oars,
I wonder why we trust boats with any cargo
that should not leave dry land: cattle and sheep;

bags of cement; mounds of coal; squeamish hearts.
Even in this murk, I know you stare at some point
just beyond my right shoulder, so I lean in.

The dock's light is a firefly and when you let go
it's so black—are we gliding or still? Forty-feet-deep,
skin of the boat so thin. We steady the bow,

unbutton each other, climb between the benches,
breathe the ruined prayer of our bodies
while nightlings chirr somber on the banks.

The Strands are Twisted, Gold and Black

My house is heaped with you. Your paintings
stave off gray walls. Your letters lap at cracks

between my drawers. Odd socks float up in
the laundry basket, on the closet floor. In my bed

I remember your last trip to town, after we said we were
through. How you slipped in beside me. Our lips.

Some nights I hear this road that joins
our doors singing miles and miles of yellow lines.

She Measures Life in Thin Slices

Never noticed in better times, these buttons she stitches,
stains she scrubs, her clothes now laundered in vast batches.

Her cats' budget kibble, spongy and light, smells like
a stockyard. They relax into it after the first pungent

bites, do their part. Meals at home every night, stir-fry, chili,
never mac and cheese. Vegetables, orange and red, crunch

as they yield to her knife, satisfy. Cost of ingredients tallied,
compared to a night at *Cher Bistro*. She fingers the ugly

jags of graphs, scans for news of war, counts the days till
she gets paid. Those droves of hungry faraway babes now

down at the City Mission, too—weak bones, no shoes,
mothers shooing flies from spoiled food. Her shame

a thin blanket, only muffles her fear. From the faucet,
glinting coins spin into the sink. Cookies stashed, cheap punch

poured for her daughter's friends. Her car screes a new noise,
like a wad of paper her stomach crumples. Under the wash

of this, a knowing—things will shift, she will not die
from it. She glimpses it like a bottle, corked and bobbing

across great waves, the glass a vernal green—inside, its ribboned
message. She wades in waist-deep as it rolls and rolls away.

Daughter at the Edge, Doan Brook Gorge

We clamber up steep roots, your hand
a small twin in mine. At the mossed crest

you find your footing, canter off. Your hips,
still slim as a boy's, but your breasts budded

in winter, the small knobs I found as you sat
on my lap still a shock. Your voice rings back

with the burble of stream as I stammer the trail.
I follow the curve of your jaw as you turn

to look back at me and when I reach you
I cradle that bone in my hand, chin to ear.

Skin, A Lament

I am vigilant now, too late. Slather
lotions, trace the terrain of my throat,
lines spraying out around my eyes,

guess the age of the youngest man
who turns my way, study light's
hard fall on my neighbor's face.

A child bends and twists, all
magical sheen, teen-aged girls
laugh past, skin like crème fraîche.

At work, necks turn: Jane's pouches,
reptilian. Against his stiff collar, Peter's
creases. Kara's, elastic, twenty-one.

I pore over photos, think genetics:
how the skin around my father's eyes
slid south and puddled; my sister, crepe

around a dimple we both inherited;
my mother, dead at thirty-four,
her face a blossom, plundered.

Song of Grief, Arranged for Woodwinds

In the dream my father is blind, my mother buys
a seeing-eye dog—it leaps and snaps—a bargain dog,

she says. Leashed, it strains as my father trips along.
Wrapped in an olive coat, my mother trails,

humming encouragement. They walk an old part
of town, storefronts tottering gray. A long front of rain

just passed through. Behind a grimy window,
shaping endless loaves of bread, a solitary baker.

Weary of wrenching, my father unleashes the dog,
which bounds toward our home. He saunters the rest

of the way alone and I wonder, could he see all along?
Skin cold and waxy, I wake. Red wail the size of my chest

vibrates behind my lips. Last week, I dreamed
my daughter and I slept side-by-side on a train

bound for Helsinki, dreaming the same dream.
Like before, I woke, my heart a wound steeped in sadness,

seeping its wet love into my lungs, my throat. It snakes in
like this, not at gravesites or sick beds,

not just after good-byes, but in the hieroglyphs of dreams
on random nights, sharp taste of walnuts, drone of a bee,

feel of a tiny shell. On a cold morning, in a crowd thick
with strangers, like the low notes of an oboe, it rises.

III

What We Know

The dead steal down to fires
we kindle in our living rooms, craving
our warmth in late autumn
when leaves are down
and they can't nestle
in branches peering out.
They come to remember taking walks,
chopping onions, washing
their hair—maybe people
we knew: mother,
first love, favorite aunt.
Or strangers: old cook, cobbler,
former mayor of our town. They don't
mind who we are or aren't.
By the third day they feel
drowsy, know it's time to leave.
On a November morning new
with snow, we trace
their footprints, light as bird tracks
though larger, leading
to a trampled place behind
the clock-tower. Here
the footprints end,
and so far, this
is all we know.

329 Miles Northeast: Woman Ponders Pain's Sweetness

Your eyes through my rear-view as I pulled away
then a hundred miles of ice between me

and the state line. A semi jack-knifed, staring back
at its tail in surprise, and a dozen slack-jawed people

in spun-out cars wondering how they got in so deep.
Gear shift humming under my hand, I dreamed

past it all, remembering your chest arced over
my back in sleep, the fire's buzz and spit.

Now I pull from my bag rumpled sweaters
and scarves, snow-wet socks dried on the hearth.

It all smells like you and I'm breathing you past
all the crushed ice, stuck cars, mile-markers

I blurred by on my way home. The only way
we can survive such a season is to cradle this space

between us as keenly as we do each other,
to love it into a smallness we can hold.

The Life I Never Lived With My Sister Pam

I miss Abilene, heat waffling off the pavement, trucks blowing through to load up on the coast, lumbering back east heavy with freight, the little silver diner where Betty slung hash and told the truckers, *I could show you boys a thing or two*, and she did. Pam and I lived at The Golden Sands, next to K-mart and Li-Wah Palace, where the locals ate hamburgers. Evenings, we perched on our cement balcony puffing Marlboro Lights, playing Wishing Well, a game we'd invented, drunk and broken-hearted over some boys. *Elephant*, I'd say. Pam: *I wish I were an elephant, I'd tear the roof off that shitty little shack down the alley, stomp the jerk who plays Slim Whitman at 3 AM.* Then *willow tree*, she'd say. Then me: *I wish I were a willow tree. I'd shoot my roots through the sewer, up into Old Lady Holeran's toilet and grab her ass, just to see her snotty face light up.* After a while we'd climb into her old red truck, hit The Camelot, a townie bar on 4th & Dixie, shoot pool with Gary, the gas station clerk and his brother Duke, who always brought his German Shepherd, also named Duke. No one else used the table, so warped with loose felt it was like playing in the grass. But we didn't mind. We didn't mind at all.

Journal Entry: Another Birthday, 3:24 a.m.

Not bad, really. Better
than last year, the hype. No new lines
that I can see.

Men still look. A teen-aged boy lagged
his family today to walk up
the stairs behind me in my skirt.

My toenails are starting to yellow,
I paint them copper or silver or gold,
no one knows.

Started running again last month.
My thighs bulge new muscles. I ice
my right knee to keep it happy.

Found a lover both sturdy
and wild, says he'll be mine forever.

Some nights, I feel my soul sprout
from the root of my body. It flames
upward, a question
in the dark.

River Song, Night Crossing

When your skin sings louder than fatigue, chants touch,
you may catalog your loves, each one's offerings: the one
you love now, taut hum of him, electric strum of his fingers;

sweet melt of the one before, all string bass and pillowed
lips; the one you tried to share, delicate ears, heavy cords
in his neck, his eyes that last time; even your ex-husband—

bulge of pectorals, burnished skin, sharp taste of his nipples.
This one's forearms; that one's jaw-line; a girl in school
you kissed just once—catch of breath as your mouths

moved apart, visible pulse in her throat. Tonight—any one
of them. You would slide to the side, hold back the sheets,
forgive that one for what each lacked or wouldn't give, ask

forgiveness for all you couldn't offer up. Warm skin, after all
is an envoy—our bodies, our souls' ambassadors. Lie back,
you'd say, lie back, let them ferry us across this empty night.

Cancerian Woman Leaves Her Home

She is saying goodbye to the house she's scorned
as cramped and gloomy—wonderful now

under her busy hands as she readies it
for those who will tend fires, curl with a book,

herb the garden. She's saying goodbye, and like
a thwarted lover her house sighs and groans,

room by room, as she dislodges what has nested
for years. It tries to show grace, to see blankets,

candles, photos, as burdens. But it was not meant
to be naked. She rescued it from lax renters,

worn floors, hued it in taupes and green leaves, sprawled
with beautiful, gentle men in every room—even

the hallway. How could the house not miss this?
Her daughter is ready to leave the penciled lines

that have notched her growing, doesn't know
her mother has traced them onto paper, will spirit them

to the new doorway. Still, here is where little heels
backed up to baseboard, little head pressed up and up.

Other ghosts: the bathroom's aqua fish rolled over white,
between attic floorboards, a letter shooshed away.

She fears her cats' ghosts will stay—has taken their ashes,
bell they rang from the doorknob. Still.

She is saying goodbye and no matter what anyone says,
she knows her house knows this.

From the dining room's old chandelier, she plucks
one crystal teardrop. No one will notice.

Her touch as she locks the back door is tender.
The tear bites her thigh through the pocket of her jeans.

Cindy Washabaugh is a poet, community artist and educator who loves living on the big waters of Lake Erie. Her mission is to connect with and support others in self-exploration, self-development and healing, both individually and in community. She has a BA in Psychology, an MA in Creative Writing and English, and has done supplemental training in Poetry Therapy. She has developed and facilitated creative writing and arts outreach programs in many organizations, with diverse populations.

Cindy has read her work widely, on her own and with her women's poetry group, *Take Nine*, at venues such as the Cleveland Museum for Contemporary Art, Cleveland Public Theater, The Cleveland Playhouse, and the Beck Center for the Arts. Her poetry and non-fiction have appeared in a variety of national and local publications.

www.ingramcontent.com/pod-product-compliance
Lightning Source LLC
LaVergne TN
LVHW041603070426
835507LV00011B/1285